Caricatures in Clay
with Tom Wolfe

Text written with and photography by Douglas Congdon-Martin

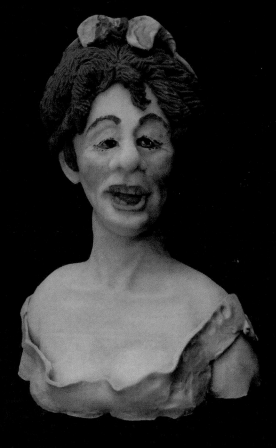

Schiffer Publishing Ltd

77 Lower Valley Road, Atglen, PA 19310

Contents

Copyright © 1995 by Tom Wolfe.
Library of Congress Cataloging-in-Publication Data
Wolfe, Tom (Tom James)
    Caricatures in clay with Tom Wolfe/Tom Wolfe: text written
with and photography by Douglas Congdon-Martin.
    p.   cm.
  ISBN 0-88740-713-7
  1. Pottery craft.   2. Pottery figures–Caricatures and cartoons.
I. Congdon-Martin, Douglas.   II. Title.   III. Title: Caricatures in
clay.
TT920.C358   1995
738.8–dc20   94-23249
                                                                CIP

Printed in China.
ISBN: 0-88740-713-7

Published by Schiffer Publishing, Ltd.
77 Lower Valley Road
Atglen, PA 19310
Please write for a free catalog.
This book may be purchased from the publisher.
Please include $2.95 postage.
Try your bookstore first.

We are interested in hearing from authors
with book ideas on related subjects.

Introduction

I don't remember when I first starting experimenting with polymer clay, but it has been part of my work for many years. Sometimes I use it just to create accessories in some of my carved scenes. Sometimes I use it to work out a challenging design before I make the first cut in the wood. And sometimes I just use it. It's fun and relaxing.

Unlike wood which creates by subtraction, clay is an additive art. The figure takes shape by adding clay in the right spots and shaping it with fingers and simple tools. For an old wood carver, this is a novel experience...and easy on the hands. Sometimes after a long day of carving, I sit down in front of the television and just play with the clay...seeing what comes out.

Clay is forgiving. If you make a mistake you can just patch it up or, if it's really bad, roll the clay into a ball and start again. That why it works well as a design tool for carvers, and why it is such a wonderful medium for those who are just starting to explore three-dimensional art.

There are several brands of polymer clay on the market, and you will need to explore them to see which works best for you. In this book I use Sculpey™ and Fimo™, which are available at most hobby and craft stores. I have found that they blend well together, and that the best qualities of each come through when they are mixed together. Be sure to read all the instructions and cautions carefully before starting.

While you can buy tools for the clay, they are easy to make from wooden dowels, a good sharp knife, and some sandpaper. I find that I always need some tool I don't have, so I'm always custom making tools.

Working in clay has brought me hours and hours of enjoyment. I hope you have the same experience.

Carving the Woman

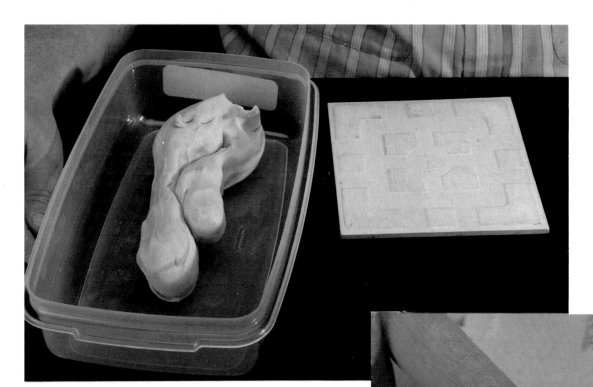

The basic clay I use for the body is a blend of Sculpey and Fimo clays. I like the elasticity of the Sculpey and the firmness of the Fimo, and they combine nicely to create a clay that I love to use. For this I am using a white Fimo and flesh Sculpey in about a half-and-half mixture. Knead it until the colors are completely blended. My work surface is a tile, because it keeps the work cool and easy to work with. The plastic container helps keep the clay moist and clean until I need it.

The tools I use are carved from various diameters of wood dowel. One tool consists of a dowel with one end cut flat and the other cupped. The flat end will make a nice hole...

and the cupped end will make a ring with a raised center. This is very useful for eyes and buttons.

A hole punched with the flat end can be filled with another color of clay, shaped in the cupped end.

Different sizes of the cupped tool allow you to make circles within circles. You could even add a third color, say for the iris of the eye.

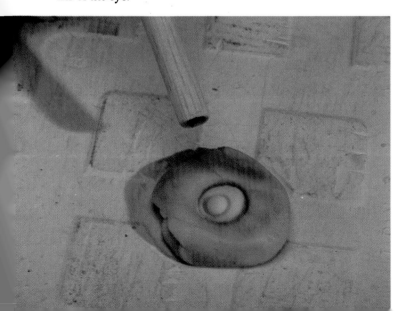

The paddle tool can be used to move and shape the clay.

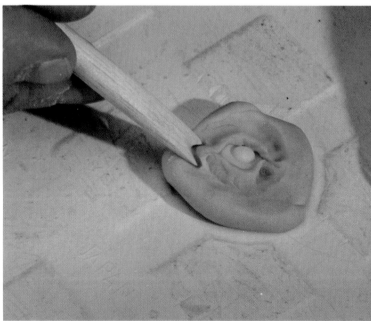

A forked end tool is also helpful, as is a point. As you model the clay you will find ideas for other shapes of tools, which you will want to create. Wood tools work well with this clay, better, I think, than the wire tools used with normal clay. As the oil from the clay is absorbed by the tool, they improve even more.

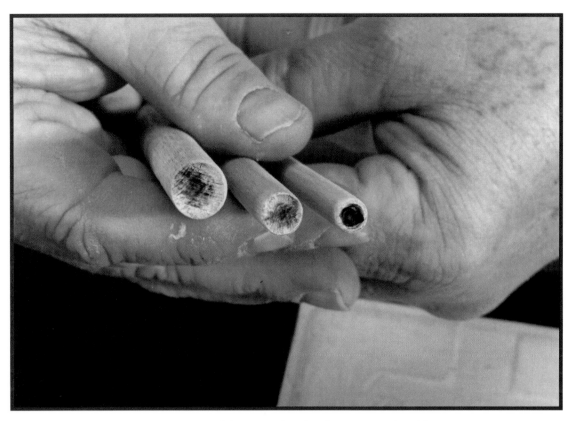

Here is a variety of the cupped tools. The cup is made with a
rotary tool ball bit.

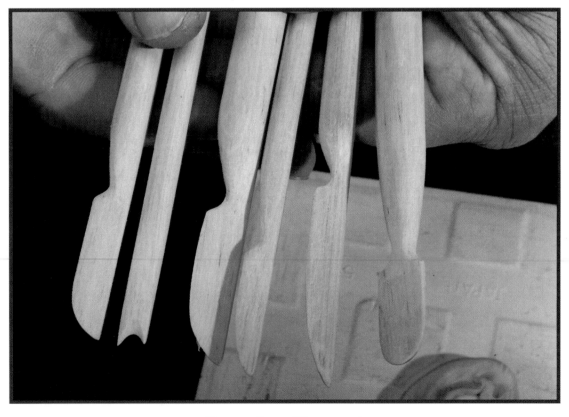

These are the paddle-type tools...

which have rounded ends that are also useful.

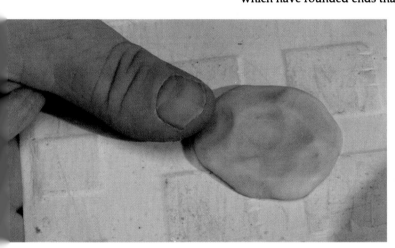

Stick a well-kneaded wad of clay on the tile. This will give a base for the additional clay to adhere to.

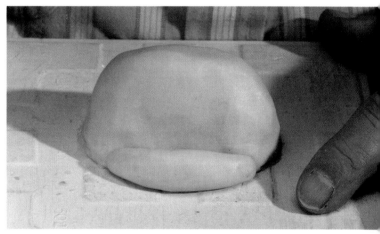

When the basic shoulder mass is built up, you can decide whether it is to be male or female. If female, you need to add the appropriate accoutrements. Add some clay to the breast area...

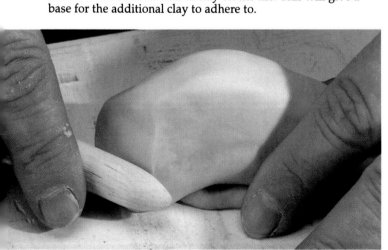

Add a lump for the shoulders of the figure. The tool is used with a rolling-pin motion. You can add to the clay without much problem, but when I can I move it around with this technique.

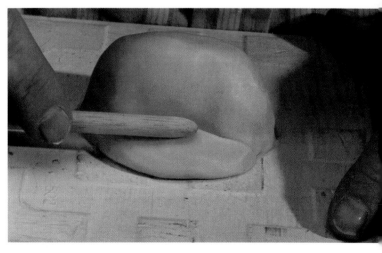

and roll it into the body.

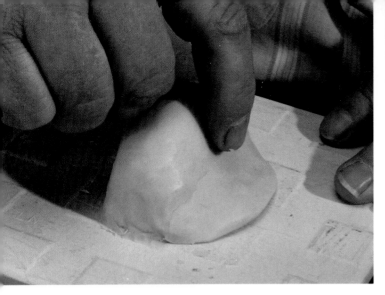

Fingers are a great tool for blending...but be sure they are clean. You don't want to have dirt permanently imbedded in the clay.

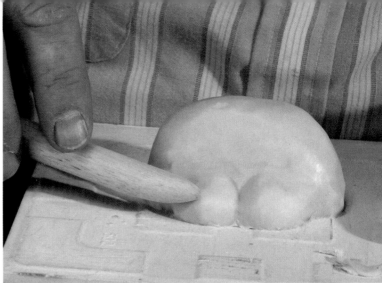

Trust your eyes. Keep moving things until they look right. This is a forgiving medium. Even after it's baked you can cut it with a knife and rework it.

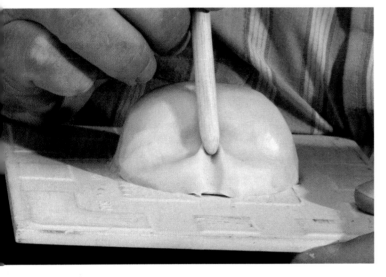

Push in with the paddle to create some cleavage.

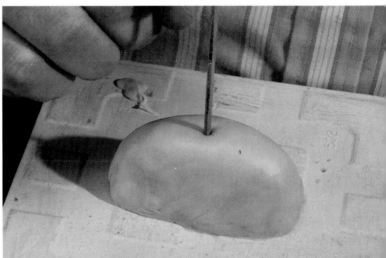

Put a thin stick through the shoulders, where the middle of the neck is to be.

Shape with the paddle, making sure the breasts are the same size. Trim or add as necessary.

Roll out a cylinder about the size you think the neck will be.

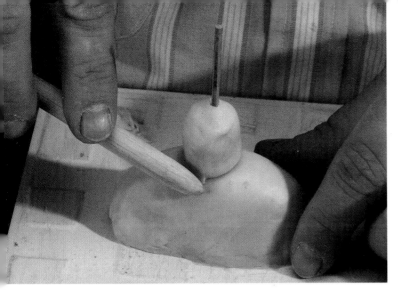

Put it over the stick and blend the neck into the torso.

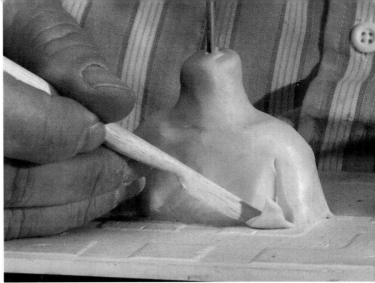

Cut out a wedge between the arm and the back, giving shape and definition to the arm.

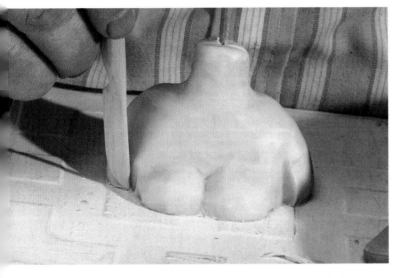

Start to define the separation between the arm and the body, moving the front surface of the arm back a little and rounding it.

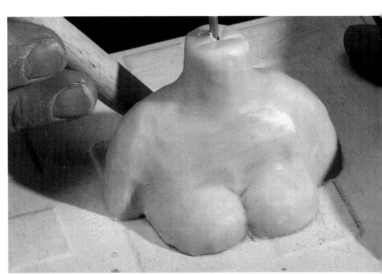

Continue to shape the torso, smoothing the surface and establishing the shoulders and contours.

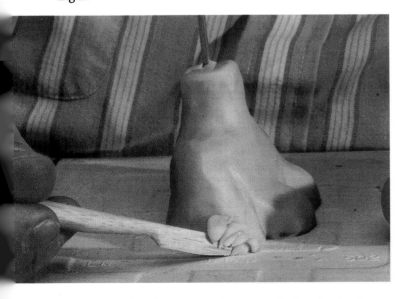

You may need to shave some of the arm off after shaping it.

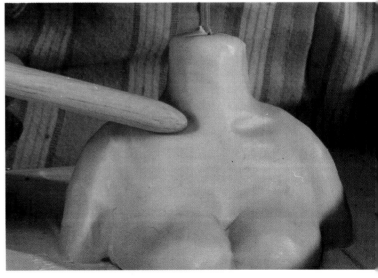

Add the line of the collar bone...

and an indentation in the center, where the muscles come in from the neck.

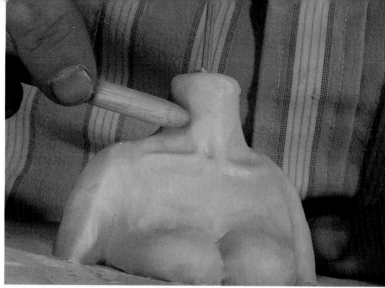

Blend the contours into the neck, bringing out the neck muscles just slightly. These muscles come from behind the jaw bone down to the center of the collar bone. Take a moment to feel them in your own neck before shaping them.

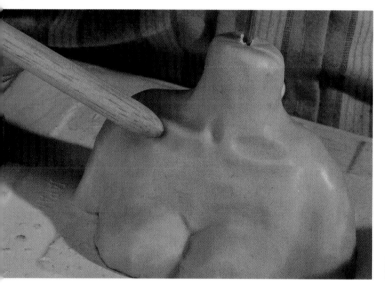

Add another, shallower indentation under the collar bone to bring it out.

As the modeling has progressed, I see that the breasts are a little large (a bad habit of mine!) so I need to reduce them a little.

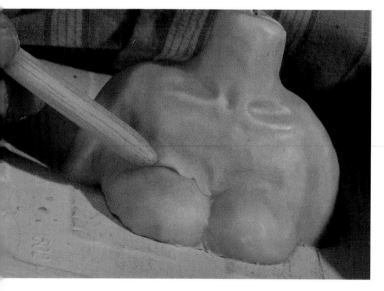

There was a slight dip in the contour above the breast so I have added some clay and am blending it in.

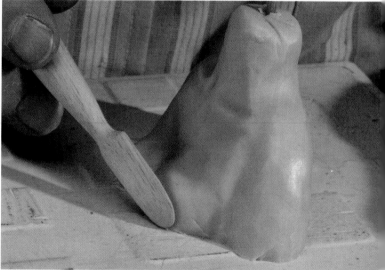

Reshape them with the paddle.

I'm going to add a little more neck. I may need to cut it off later, but that's easier than adding more.

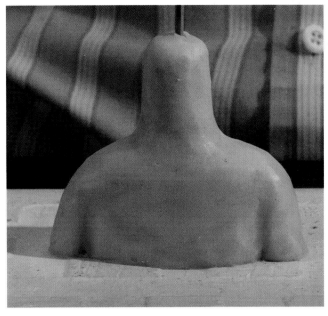

Ready for the oven.

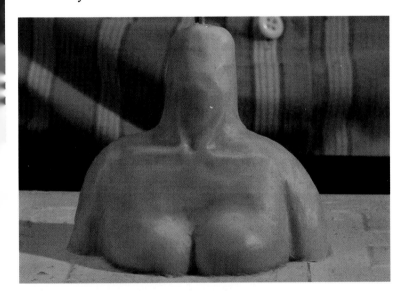

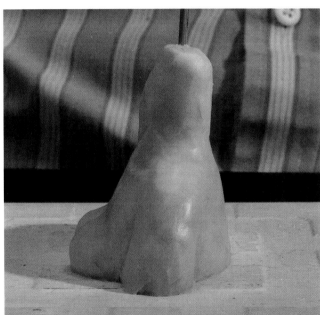

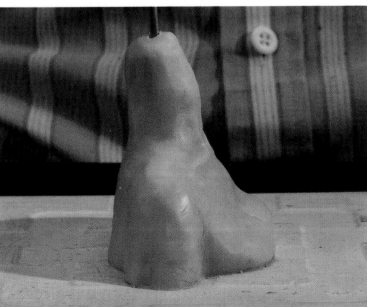

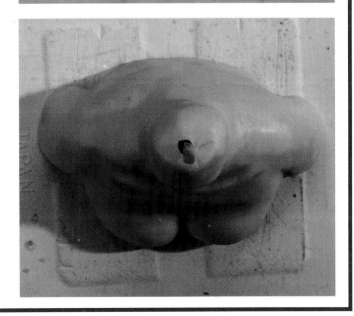

Roll a ball for the head.

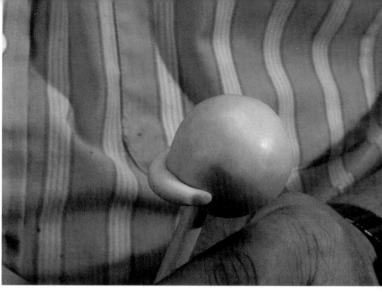

and add it to the head.

By putting the head on a stick and can smooth it and shape it more easily.

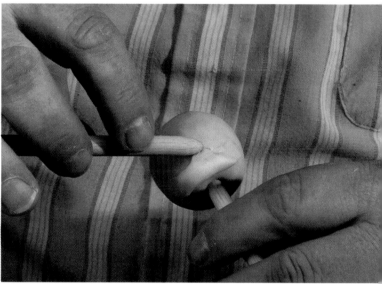

Blend it into the face.

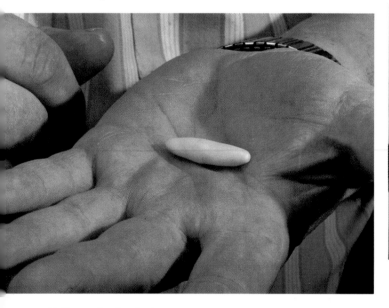

Roll a snake for the jaw...

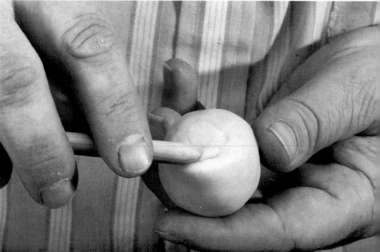

Add pieces where you need them, like here under the chin. The good thing about the clay is that you can add it anywhere you want, and if you change your mind you can take it right off.

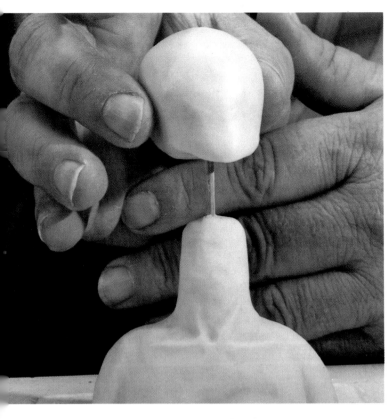

When the body is cured place the head on it.

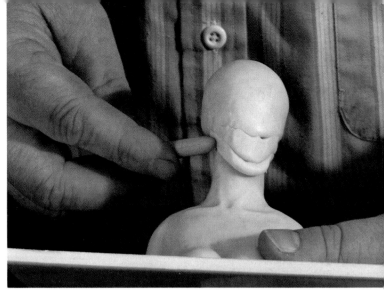

Blend in the added piece.

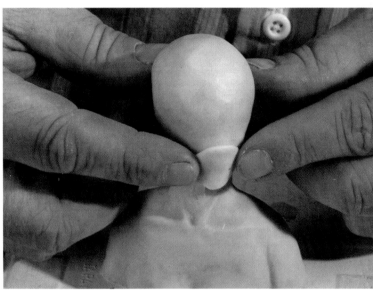

Now I need to build up the face by adding clay.

The neck is a little long looking. To make it look right I could trim the neck or make the face longer, which is what I am doing by adding to the jaw.

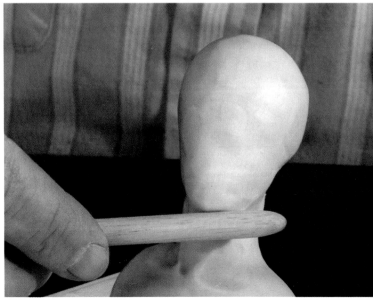

Roll the clay to shape it.

13

If you need to move a mass of clay from spot to another, you can pick up a little by rolling the tool backwards as you push the clay toward the area you wish to fill.

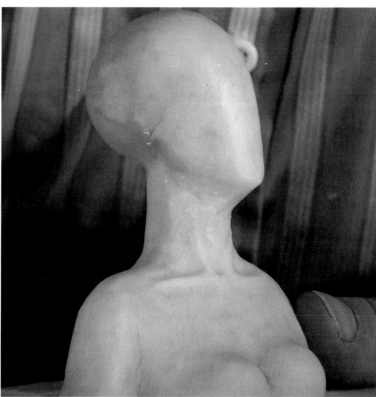

Progress.

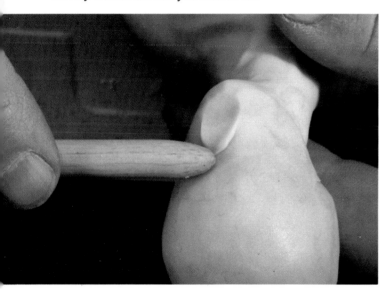

At the end of the stroke, roll the tool forward to deposit the clay where you want it.

If you discover a high place in an area that is already cured, like here on the neck, you can simply trim it off with a knife.

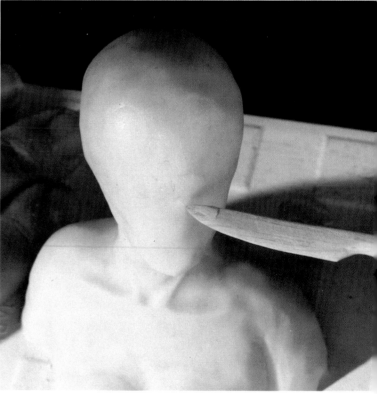

The eye line is about half way down the face. I make a small indentation there so I can see it while I make the sockets.

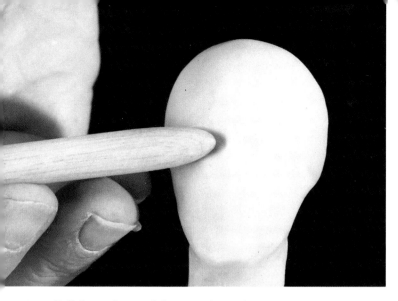

Roll the tool up and down in the socket to form it. This raises the eyebrow and the cheek bone.

and stick it in the right place.

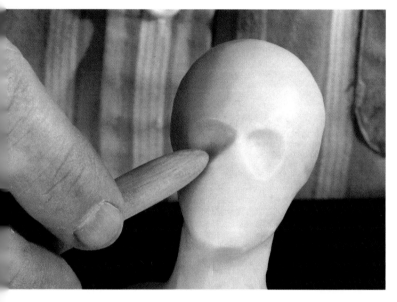

The result.

Make sure it is well set and blend it with the face before shaping it.

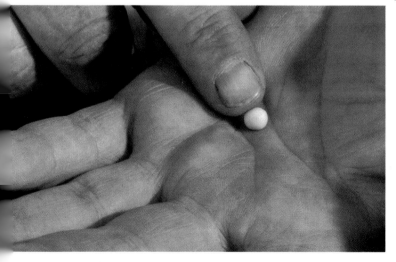

Because this is a caricature I'm going to add some material for the nose. If it were a realistic figure, I would probably simply push some material up. Roll a small amount of clay into a ball...

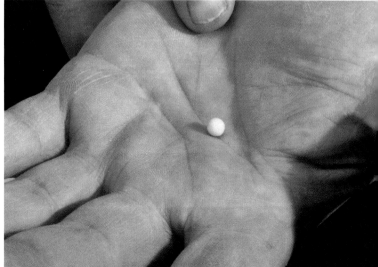

For the nostril form a ball...

and cut it in half. This helps make both sides equal.

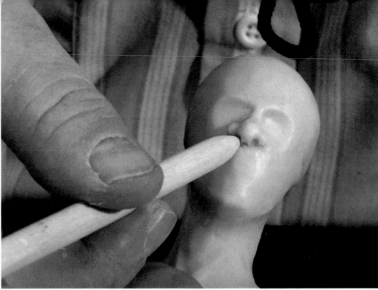

Form the nostril using the pointed end of a tool.

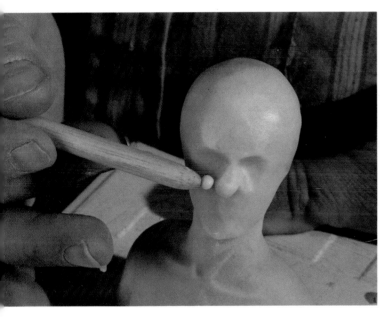

Apply the halves to the nostril...

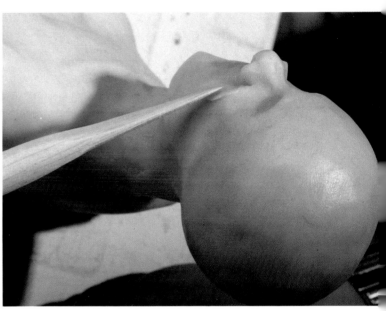

Move some of the material from the top lip over to the cheek.

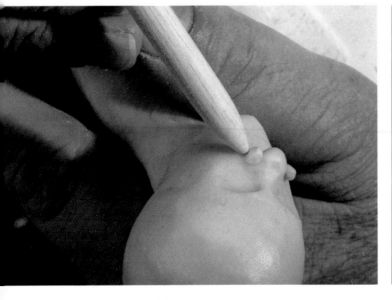

and shape and blend them in.

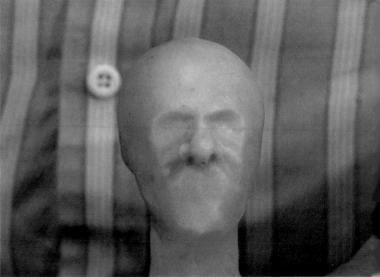

This begins to create the cheek line.

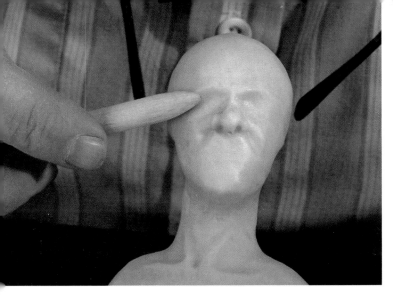

Open the eye sockets a little more, rounding them into the temples.

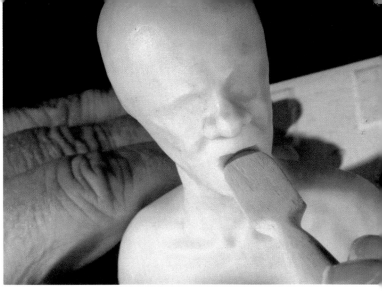

and push down to open the mouth. The downward push actually opens the jaw some too.

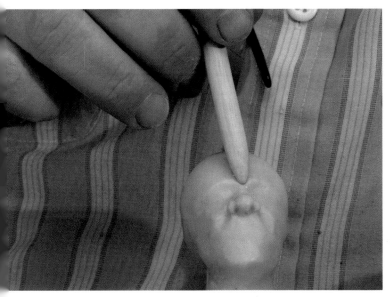

Put a small indentation between the brows.

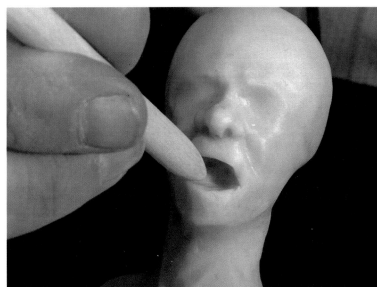

With a rounded end of the tool, smooth things out.

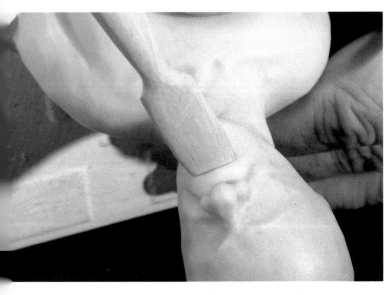

Go into the mouth with a paddle tool, about half way between the nose and the jaw. Lift up...

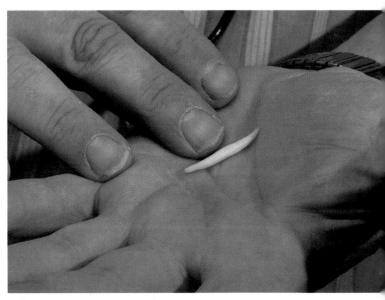

Roll a snake of white clay.,...

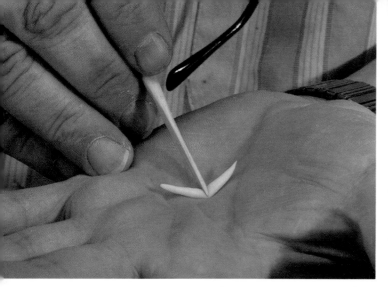

Cut it in half to get two equal pieces.

A few lines with the end of your knife shaped tool and you have the uppers.

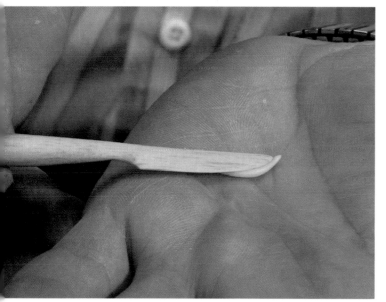

Roll one half out and flatten it down to create the teeth.

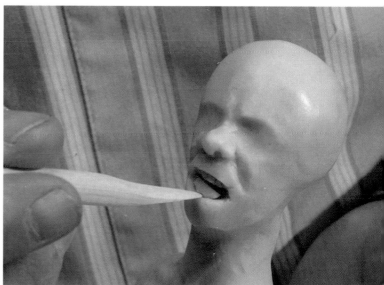

The bottom teeth are a little smaller, but are done in the same way. Lay them in...

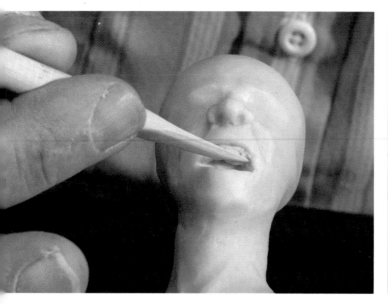

Place the teeth in the mouth and shape.

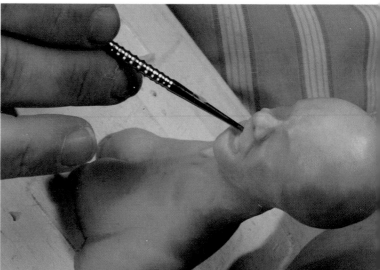

and shape them...

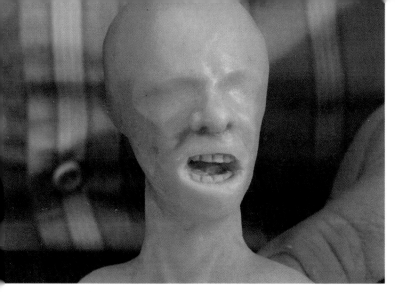

for this result.

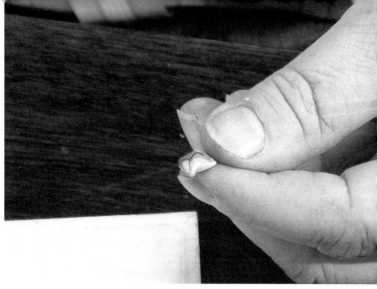

A little peach clay plus a dab of red gives me a nice lip color. Knead the clay until the colors are well mixed.

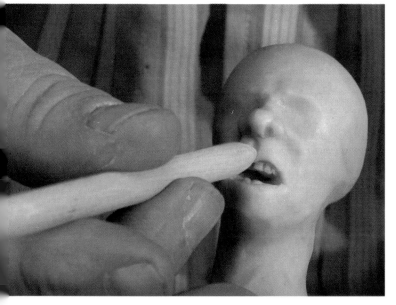

Put the "angel's fingerprint" between the lip and the nose...

This color is about what I want for the lips.

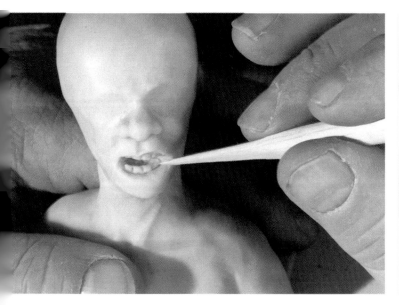

then lift up the sides of the upper lip to shape it.

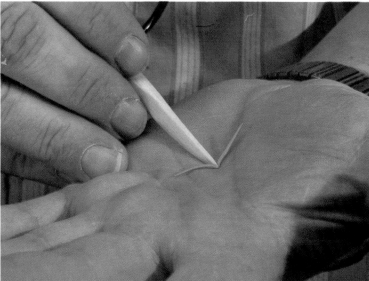

Roll it into a thin strip and cut it in half.

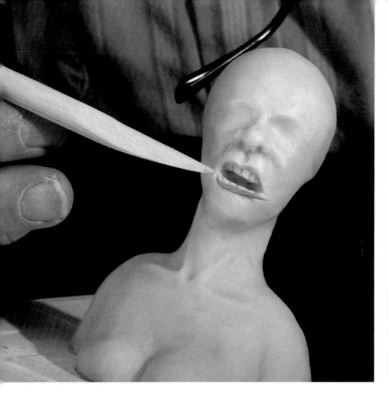

Apply it to the lip and mash it in.

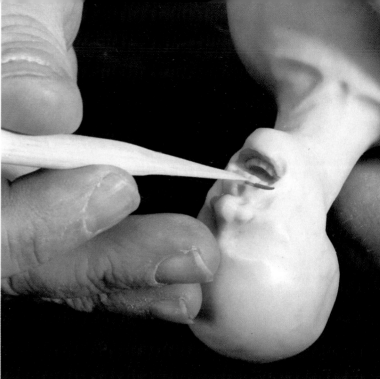

The upper lip is done the same way.

Progress.

A little dark red is used for the tongue. Shape it...

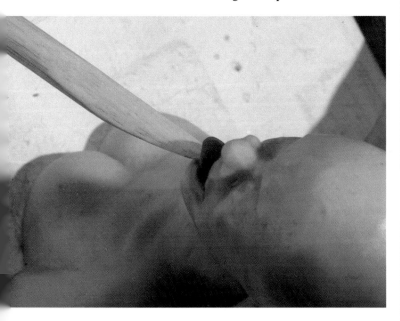

and put it in the mouth.

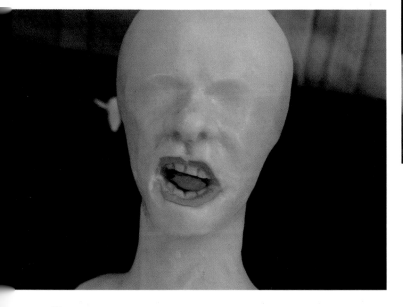

Progress.

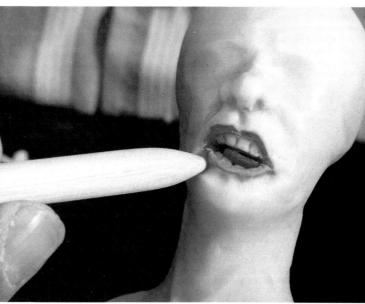

Close the mouth a little and begin to add some character by setting a contour under the lower lip.

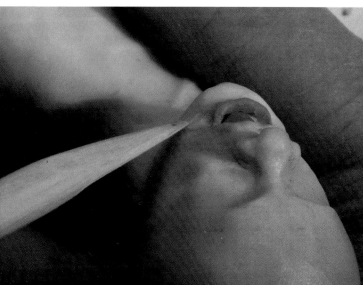

I need to build up the face a little beside the mouth and blend it in.

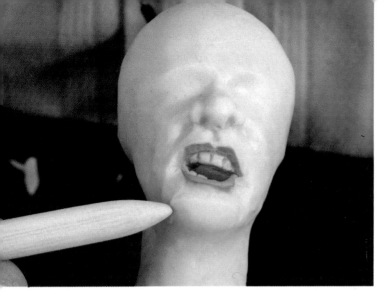

Add some character lines down the side of the chin.

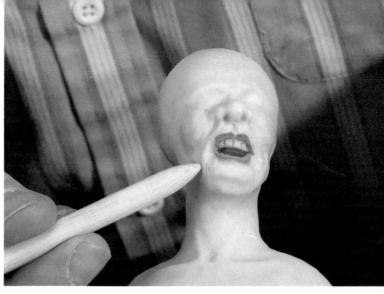

Bring a line behind the cheek line, to add some more character.

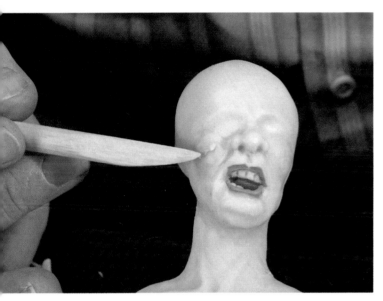

Apply a speck of pure flesh tone Sculpey and blend it into the cheek give it a blush tone.

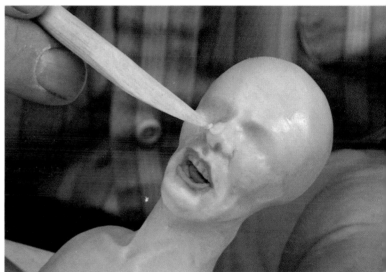

Add another speck of flesh tone Sculpey to the tip of the nose...

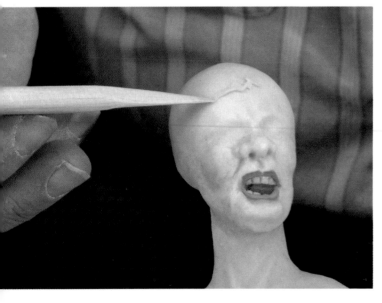

Do the same thing in the forehead.

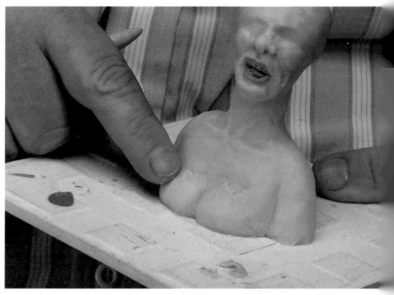

and to the top of the breasts.

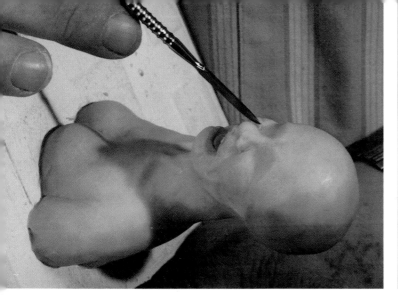

The nose is a little large, even for a caricature, so a little more plastic surgery is in order.

it is more in keeping with the face.

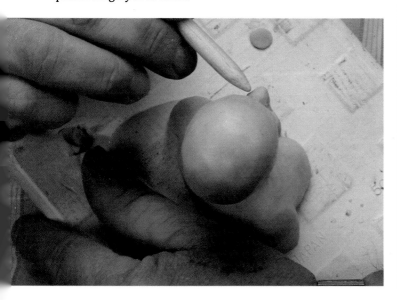

After the removal, you need to smooth things up.

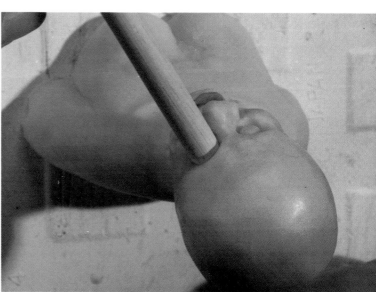

Use the cupped tool to form the round of the eyeball...

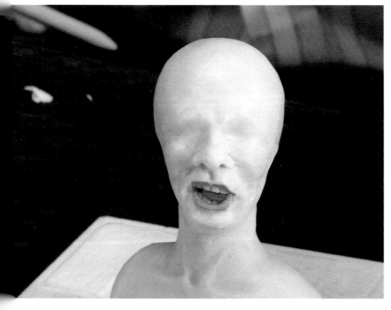

The result. While still a caricature...

for this result.

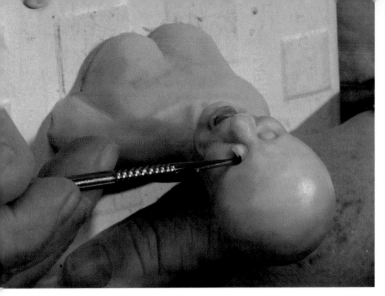

I'm going to dig some of the eyeball out so I can replace it with white. Without doing this, the additional white would make the eyes bulge.

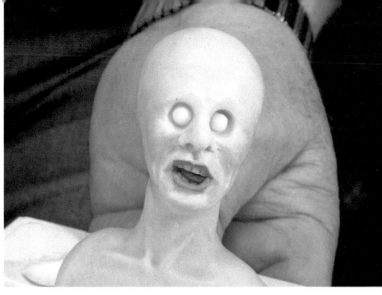

The "Little Orphan Annie" look.

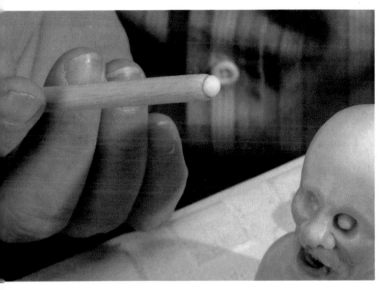

Roll a small ball of white and hold it in the end of the cupped tool...

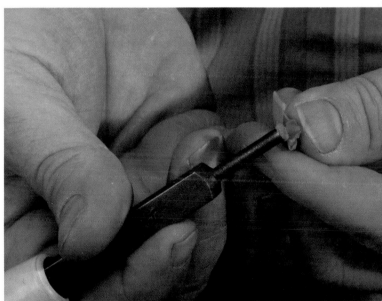

Work the iris color into the cup of a nailset or eyepunch.

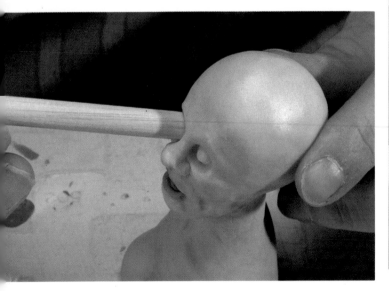

to insert it into the eye socket.

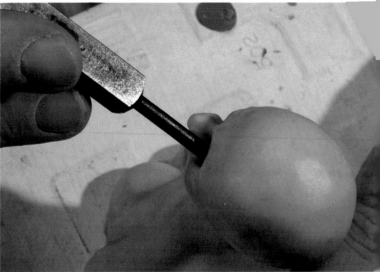

Apply it to the eye and twist lightly until the iris is set in the eyeball.

The result.

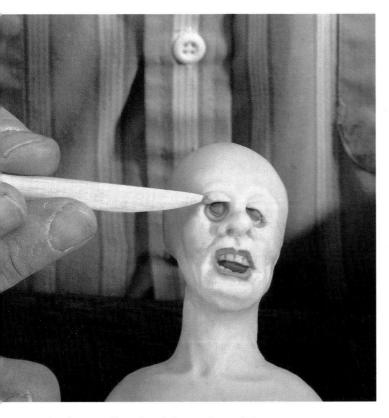

Apply a small snake of clay to the eyelid.

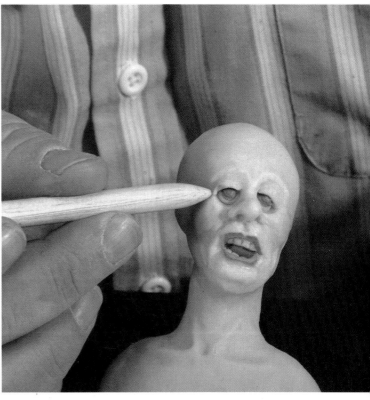

Work it into shape.

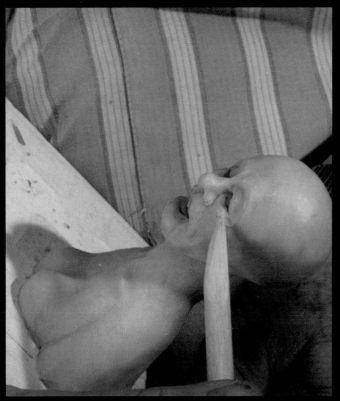

Follow the same steps for the lower lids.

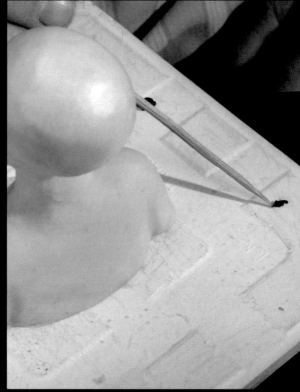

Pick up a speck of black on the end of a toothpick or bamboo skewer....

Add crow's feet and other character lines to the eyes.

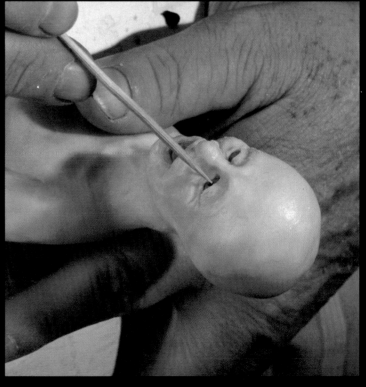

and apply it to the pupil of the eye.

Progress on the eyes.

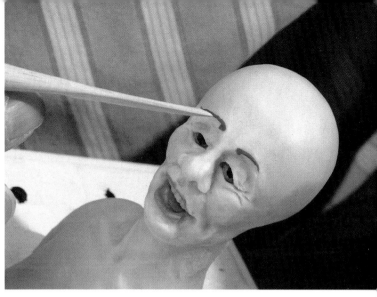

Do the other side in the same way.

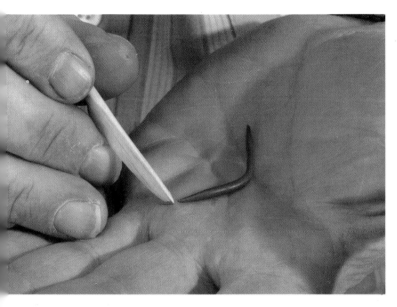

Roll a snake of the hair color and cut a small piece from the end for the eyebrow.

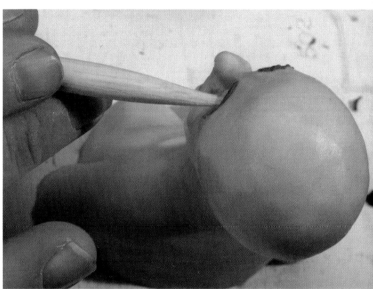

Adjust and shape the eyebrows...

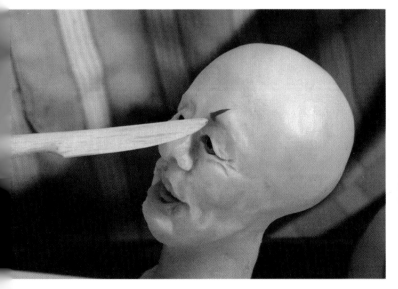

Put it in place with the thick end at the inside corner and work it out.

until you get a result you like. It would probably be wise to bake the piece again, to cure the head.

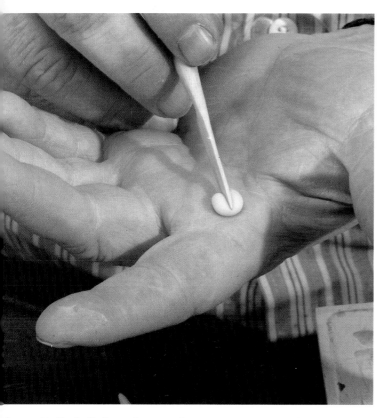

Roll a ball about the size of two ears and cut it in half.

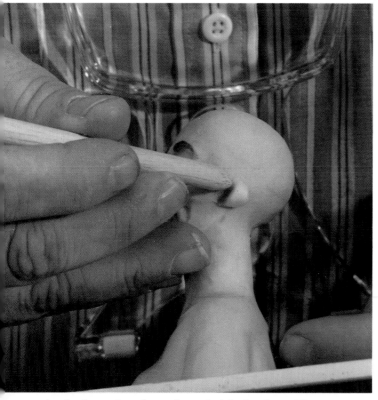

Apply the ear just above the end of the jaw bone. The top should align with the eye. Work it so it joins smoothly with the head. When joining the soft clay to the hardened clay you want to get a good connection all around. If a piece should fall off tacky super glue will hold it back. **Only do this after the final baking.**

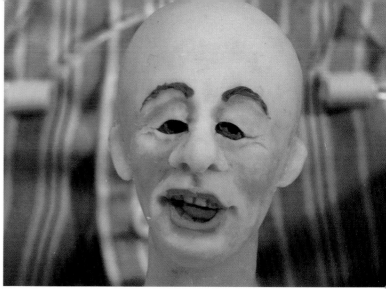

Establish the basic shape of the ear...

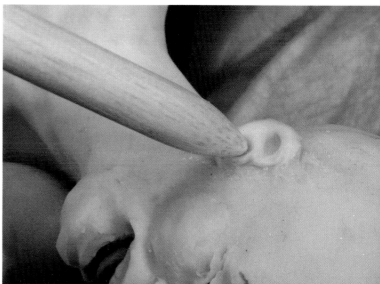

and add details to the ear. The basic detail starts with two indentations above each other. From there you need to feel your own ear to get the sense of how an ear is built.

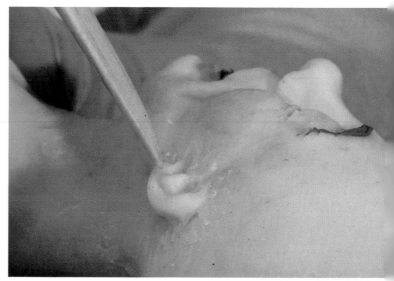

Gently add the line around the outside of the ear.

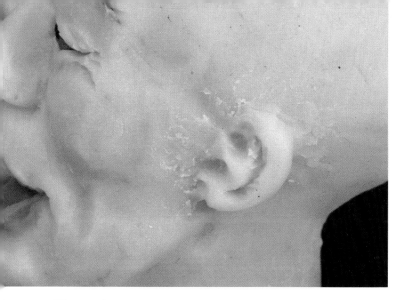

The result. The ears are so fragile that it is best to harden them in the oven before continuing.

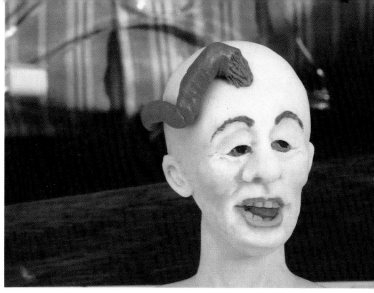

The hair is laid on a piece at a time. I often start here at the front. Reference to a picture is most helpful in setting a hair design...especially if the figure is a period piece, as this one is.

Mix up some compound for the hair. This is the color of the eyebrows with a little yellow added to lighten it. The hair is usually a shade or two lighter than the eyebrows.

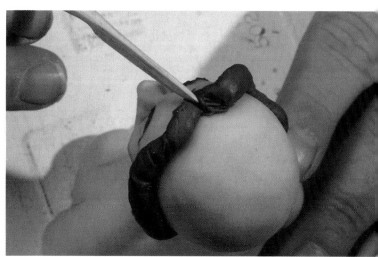

Add a second strand, working it into the first and smoothing it into the scalp. You want it to be well attached to the scalp.

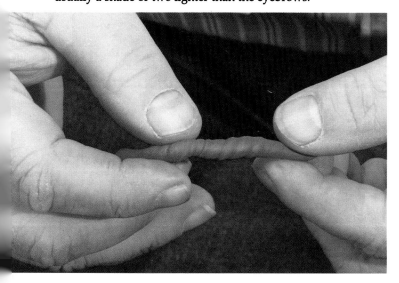

The hair curls are made from a snake of compound that is twisted.

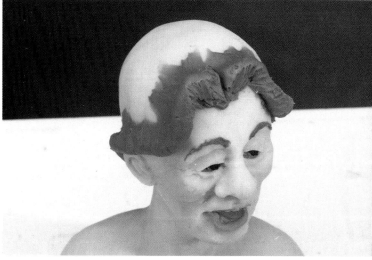

You can get the best adhesion by spreading the compound with your finger. Do this behind the hair line, where it will be covered by the next strand.

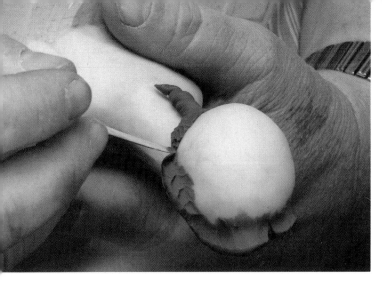

I'm going to add a pin-curl in the back and continue the outside ring of hair.

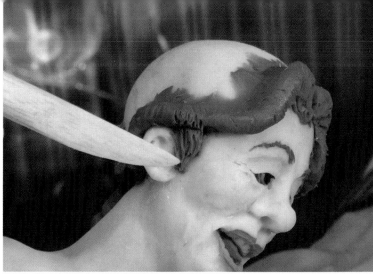

Shape and add some hair lines. I would have rather had the twist, but the compound didn't stick well and I had to push it harder, distorting it. The hair lines make it look pretty good, though.

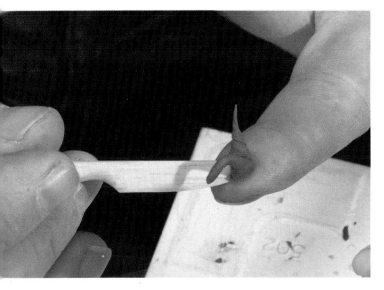

Another curl will go in front of ears. Twist a lock and cut it in half.

To fill in the hair I begin by working in three curled strands.

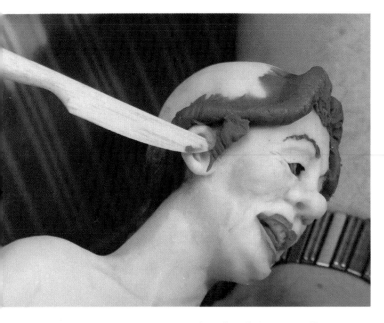

Apply it in front of the ear and push it down so it adheres.

As you work add the lines of the individual hairs.

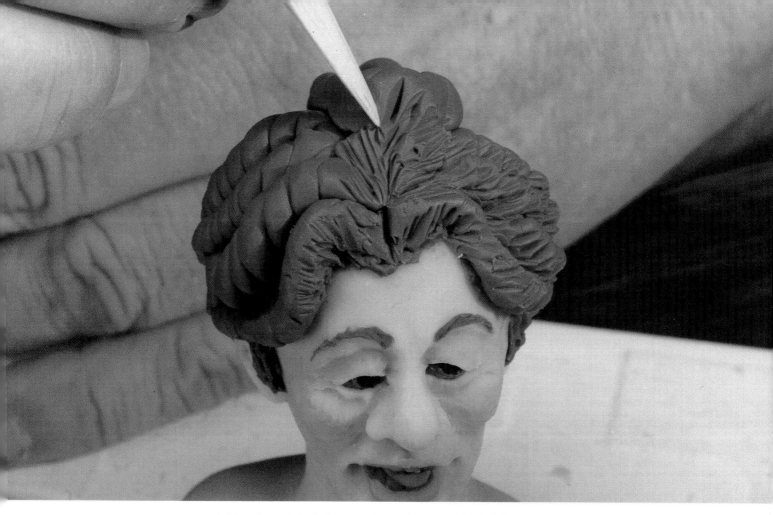

Add and work the hair one curl at a time, until the hairdo is complete.

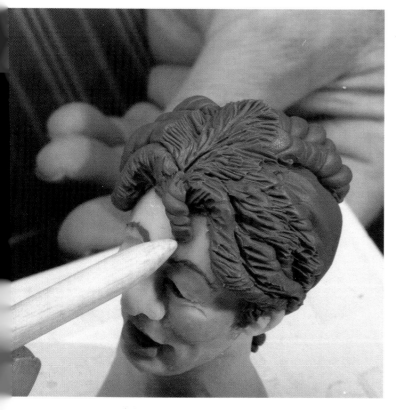

A curl in the front adds life to the face.

A subtle touch, like splitting the end of the curl, is the little bit that makes all the difference. Trust your eye.

Now that the major movement of the hair is established you can go back and add details.

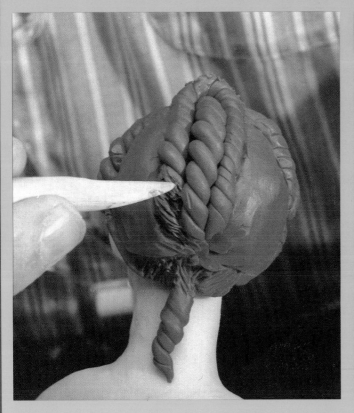

I need to add a couple more curls to the back.

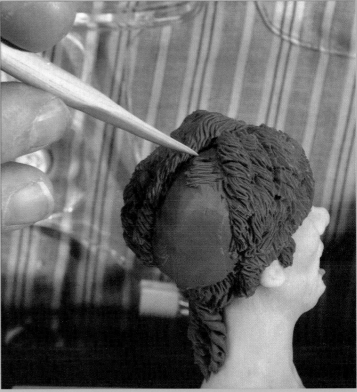

The large areas of hair need lines to make it look as though it is sweeping around the head.

Progress.

The result.

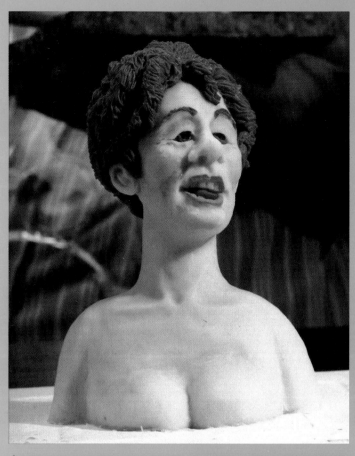

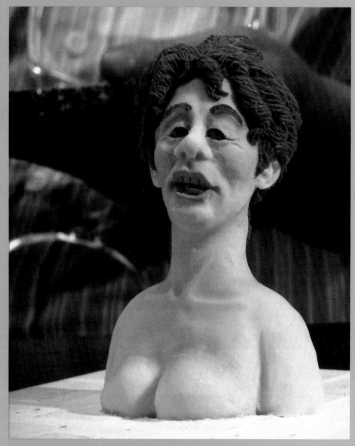

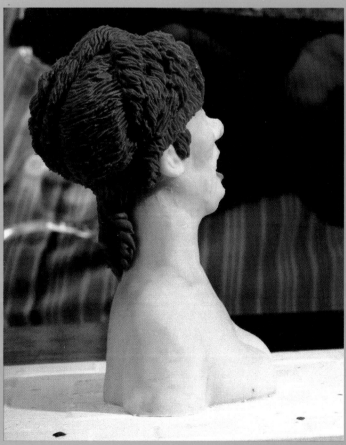

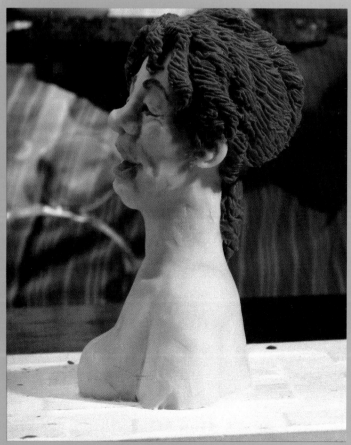

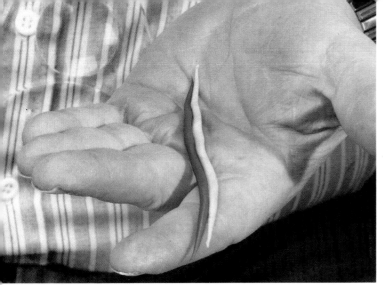

To get some striped pattern in the cloth take two snakes of compound...

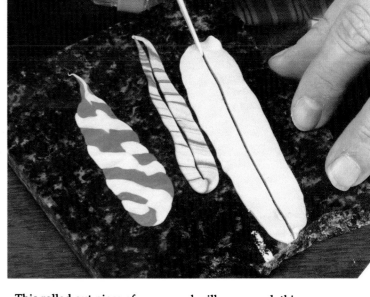

This rolled out piece of compound will serve as clothing fabric. You need to work the material on a smooth surface like glass or marble, so it won't stick.

and twist them together.

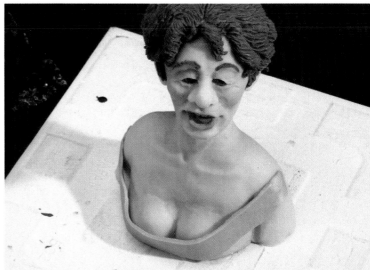

Drape the fabric around the bust.

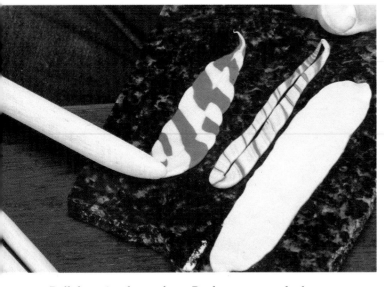

Roll the twisted strand out. By the two examples here you see the variety of effects you can get.

Use the tools to work the fabric, and give it detail.

With two tools you can create a nice folded effect around the top of the dress.

Add ribbons to the hair...

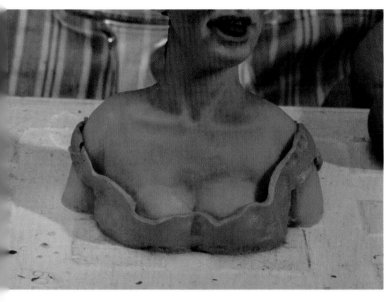

This is the effect in the front...

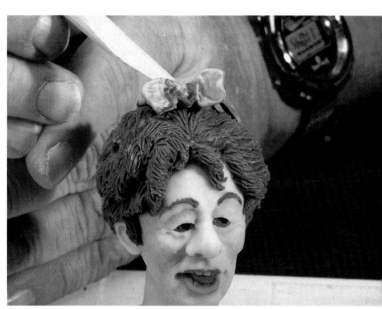

coming to a bow at the top.

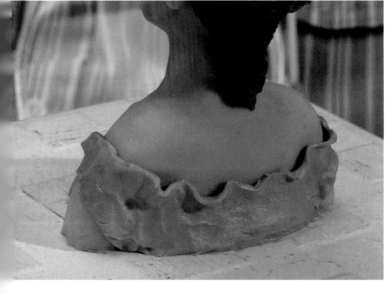

and the back.

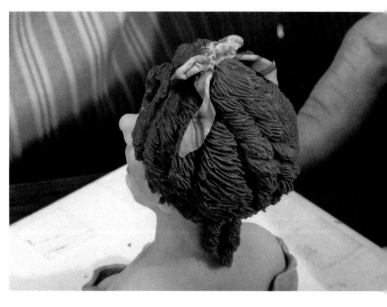

A little twist to the ribbon gives it more movement.

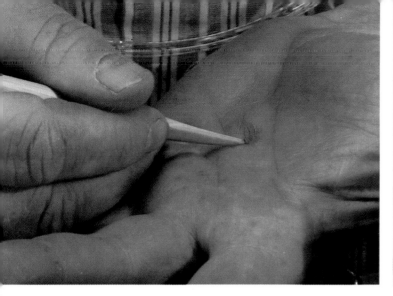

The cheeks need a little more color, so I mix some red with the flesh tone compound...

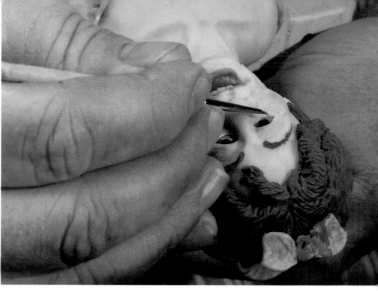

The iris is a little dark, so I'm adding a little light blue paint to the bottom edge of it. I use tube paint for this.

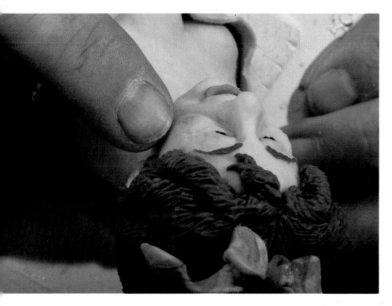

and apply it with a finger, just like you would with rouge.

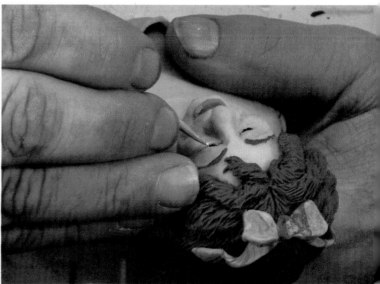

A glint of white paint is applied with a tooth pick or bamboo skewer. It should go right beside the pupil, or, if you can, between the pupil and the iris.

Ready for baking.

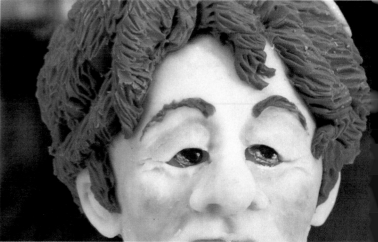

The result. The colors should be in the same positions in both eyes.

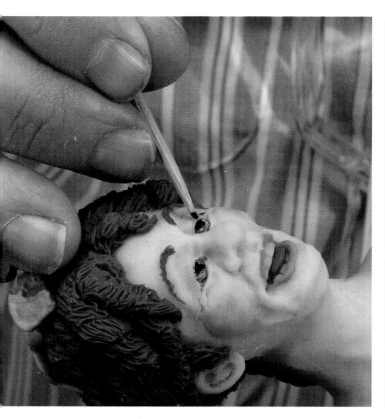

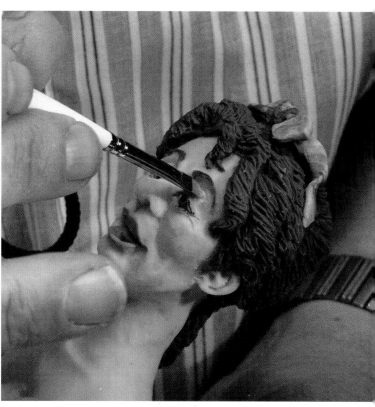

This can be disasterful, but I want a hint of an eyelash along the edge. I do this with the bamboo skewer for greater control of the paint.

Finally add a little tint of blue eye shadow above the eyes. Apply a small amount light blue paint and feather it out with a dry brush.

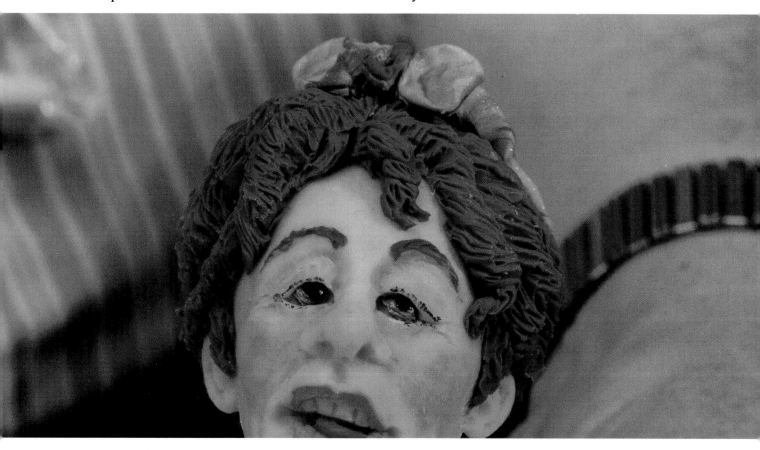

The result.

Finished.

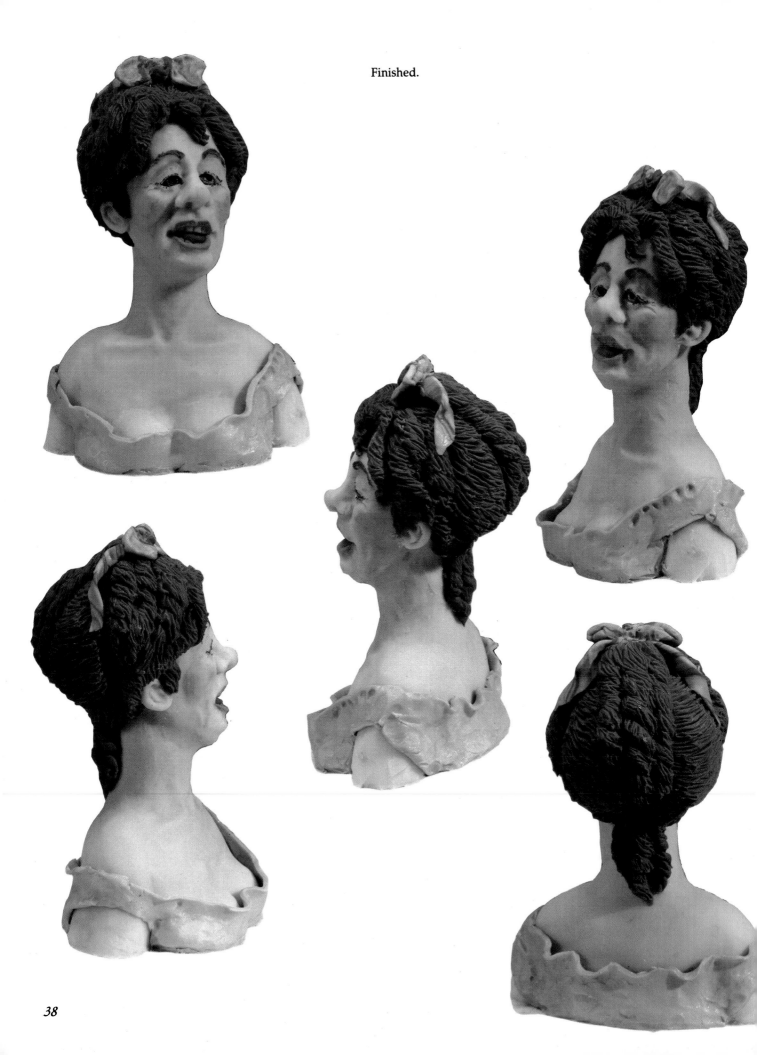

Carving the Man

The male figure starts much as the female did. Work the torso
and head to about this shape.

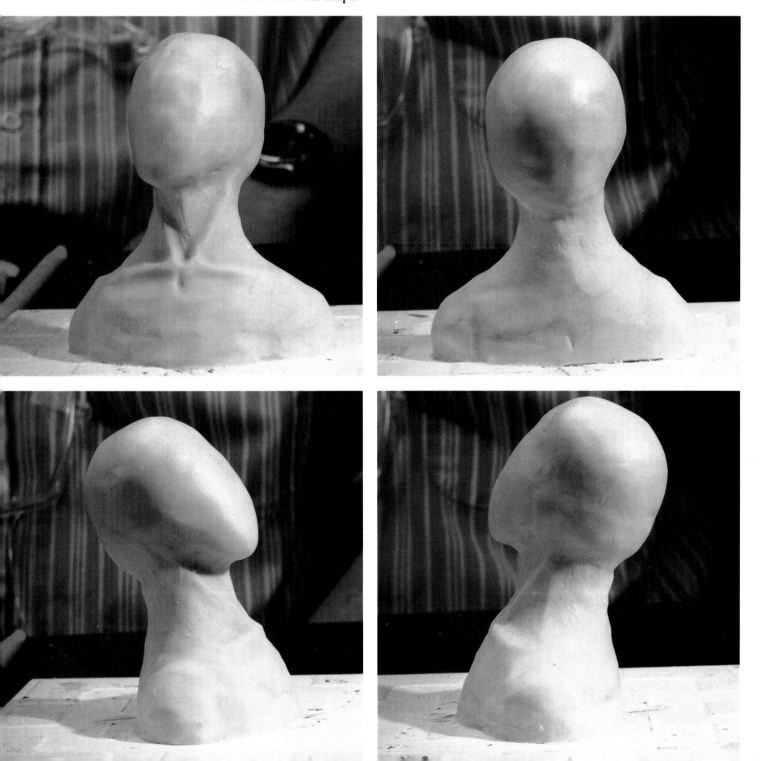

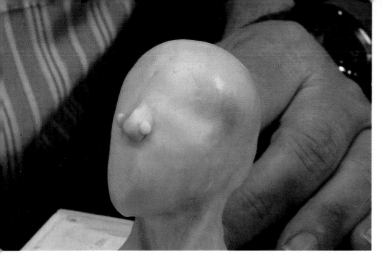

Add clay for the nose and smaller balls for the nostrils.

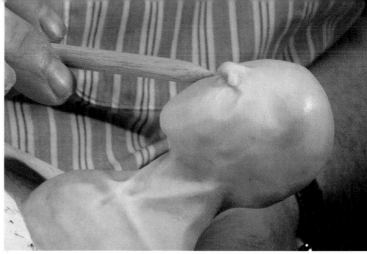

Lift the cheek line from the upper lip...

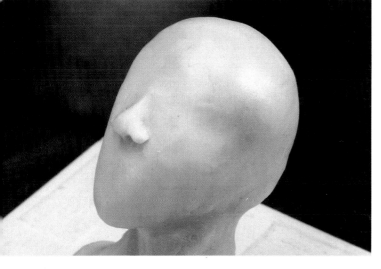

Shape and blend the nose.

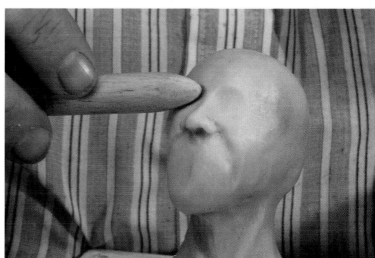

and form the eyesockets.

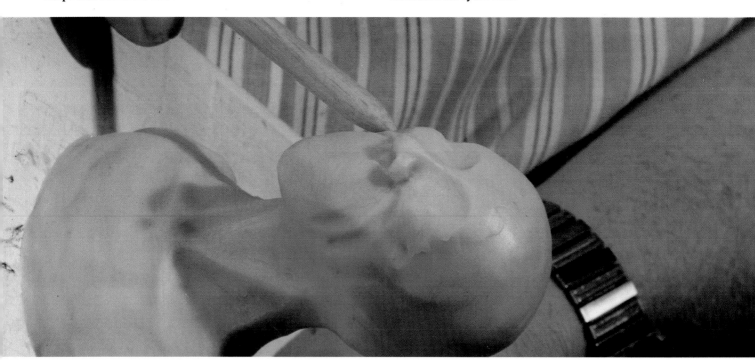

Build up the cheek bones and get some movement in the face around the moustache.

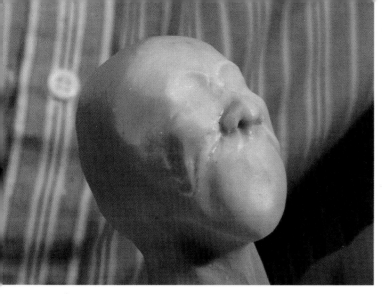

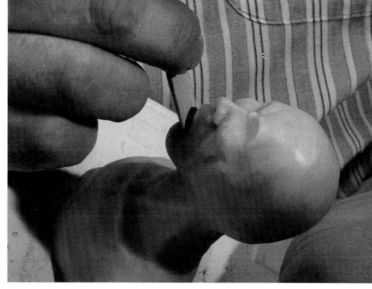

and down.

Nostrils will take us to about this point.

The yawning result.

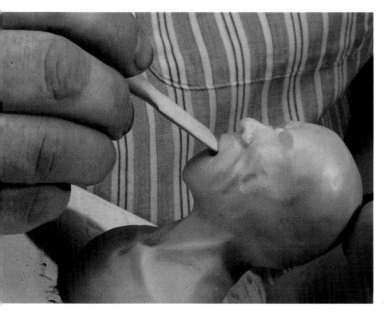

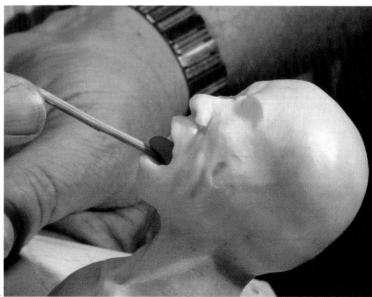

Open the mouth with a paddle, pushing up...

Form a tongue and insert it in the mouth.

Flatten and shape a snake from white compound to form the teeth.

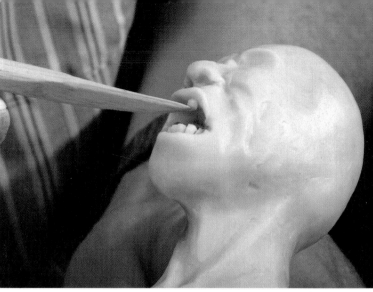

A single upper tooth will give a nicely comic look with the moustache.

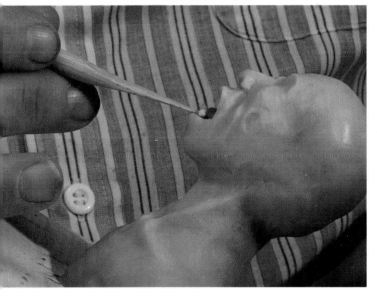

Insert it in the lower jaw.

Roll a snake of pink for the lip.

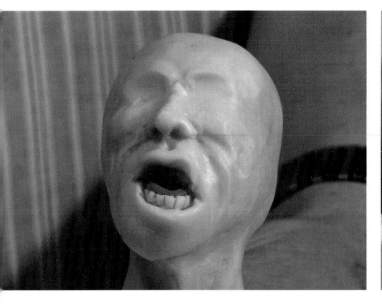

Separate the teeth for this result.

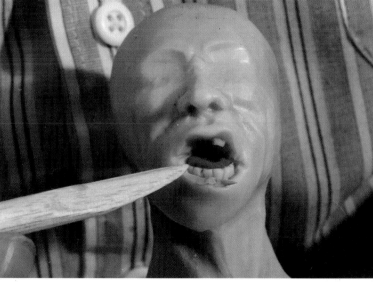

Work it into place on the lower lip...

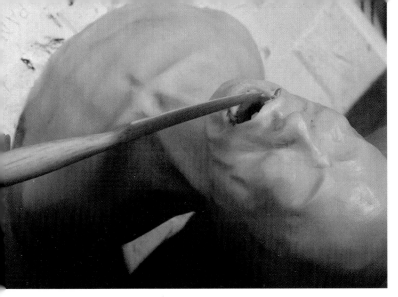

and repeat on the upper.

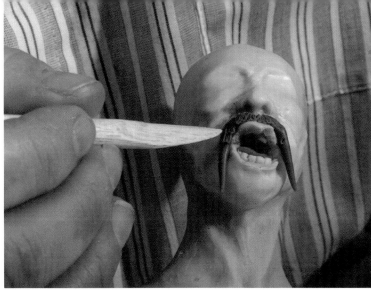

Work the two halves of the moustache onto the face.

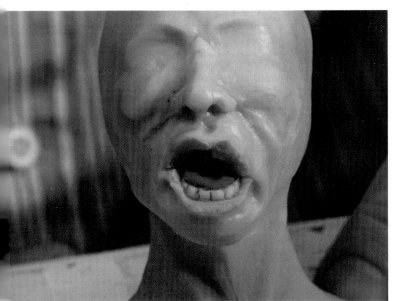

Progress on the mouth.

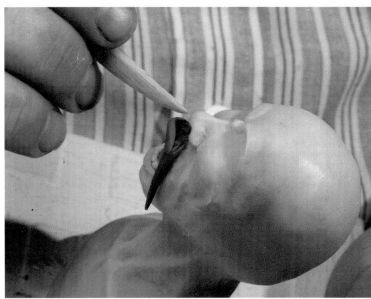

The moustache needs to be bushier, so I simply add some more and work it in.

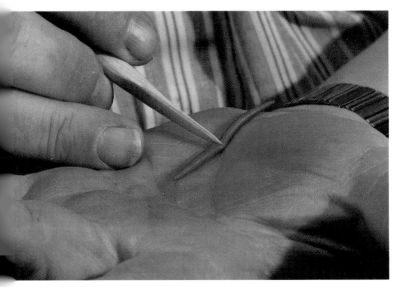

I've mixed copper and yellow to get a light hair color. Roll snake of it for the moustache.

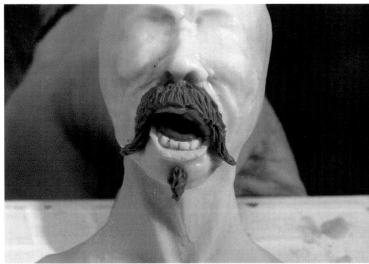

The fixed moustache plus a little goatee. Remember to add the hair lines to both.

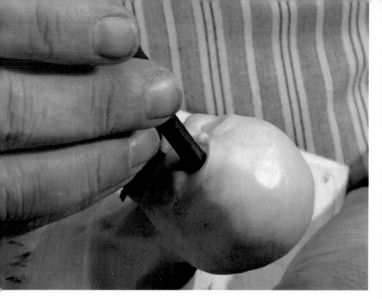

Form the eyeballs with a metal or a wooden eyepunch.

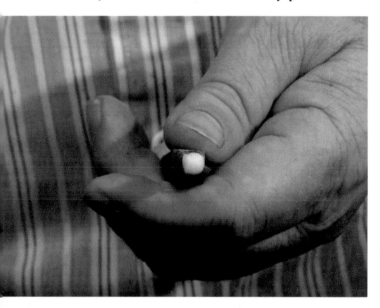

Fill the end of the punch with white compound...

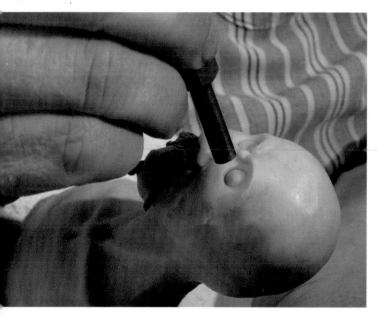

and transfer it to the eye.

Progress.

Pick a smaller punch to form the iris and fill it with colored compound. I've chosen brown.

44

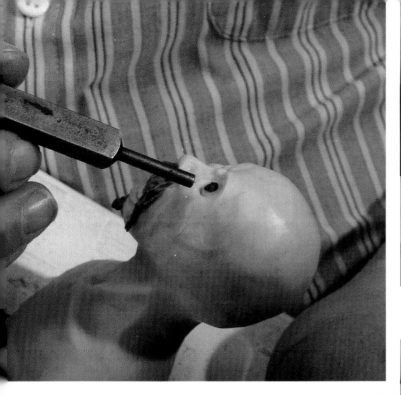

Transfer this to the eyeball.

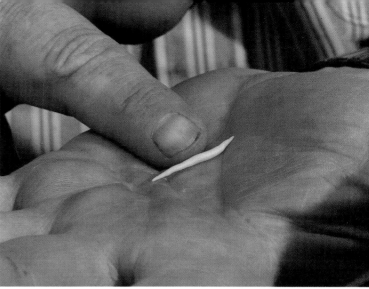

Roll enough flesh colored compound for two eyelids into a snake.

Put it in place over the eyeball...

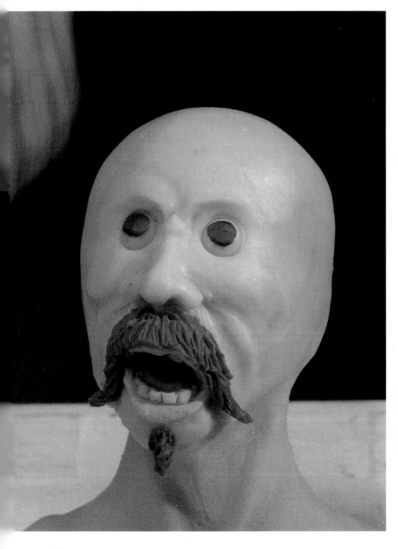

Progress.

and blend it for this result.

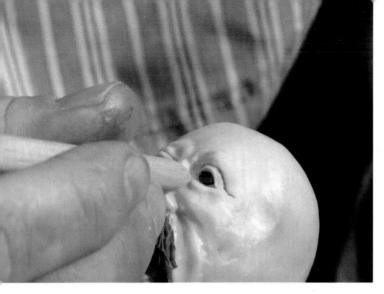

For the bottom lid, we have enough face material to simply roll it up to form the lid.

The result.

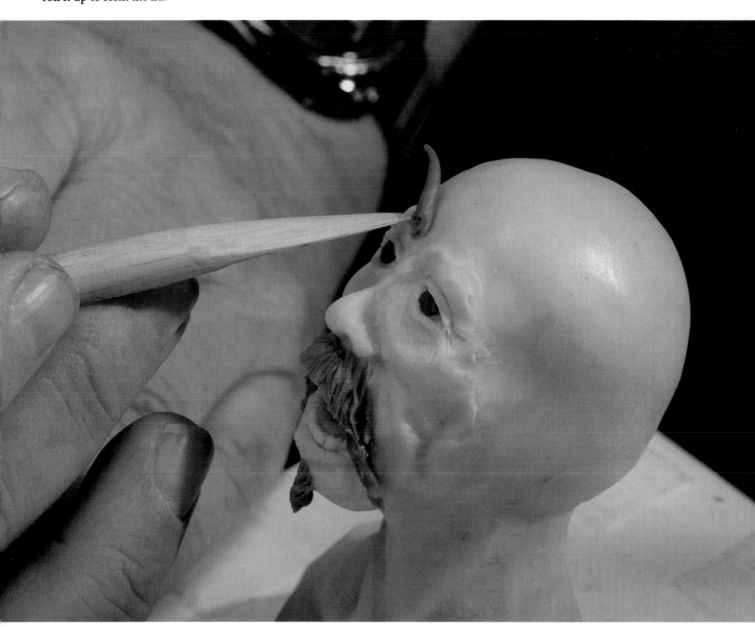

Apply the eyebrows to the brow.

Shape them to the brow line and blend with the face.

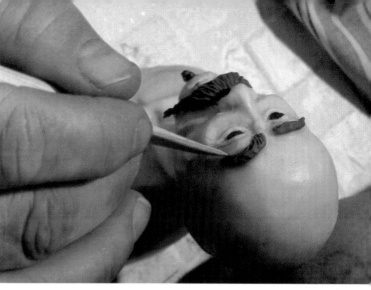

Bush the eyebrows up with hairlines coming from the center over and down.

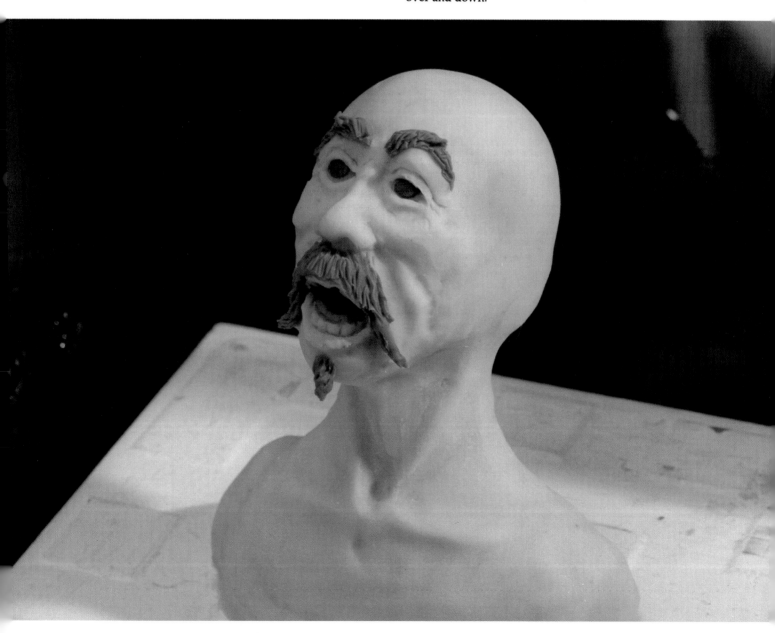

Ready for baking.

Begin the top hat by forming a cylinder of black compound.

Wrap a snake of compound around the bottom of the hat to form the brim.

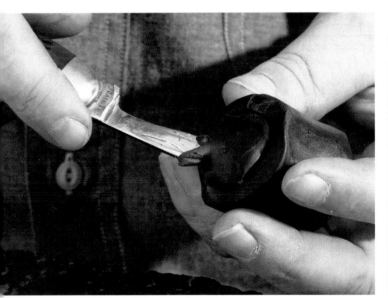

Cup out an area to go over the head.

Work the brim into the crown of the hat, as you begin to flatten and shape it.

Place the hat on the head and work it in. The rakish angle seems right for this dandy.

Shape the brim, then add the lines of the hat band.

Ready for baking.

Cut a ball of flesh in two to form the ears.

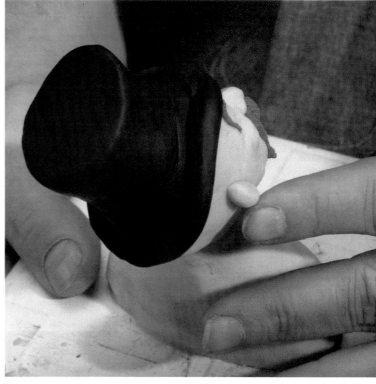

Attach the ears about halfway between the eyes and the back of the head.

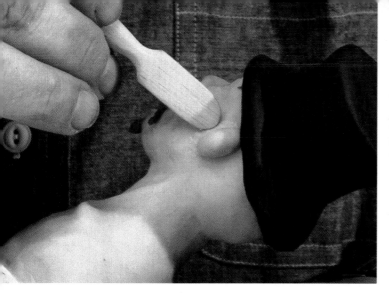

Stick them down with the paddle tool.

Do some final shaping for added realism and bake the head.

Size and shape the ears.

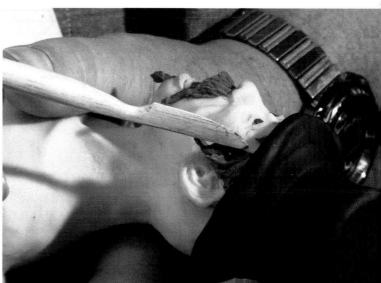

The under layer of hair is brown...

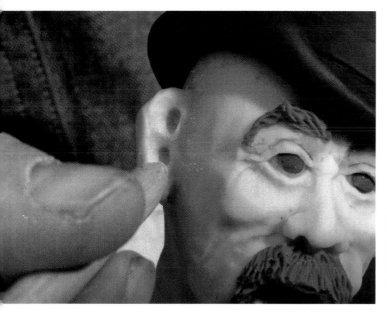

Put holes in the top and bottom of the ears.

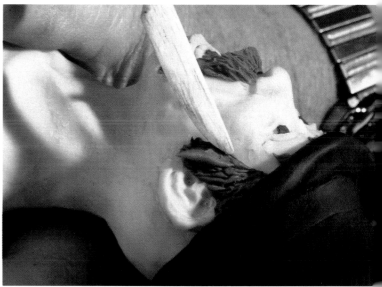

with highlights of the lighter eyebrow color added on top.
This second color is only a shade or so lighter for effect.

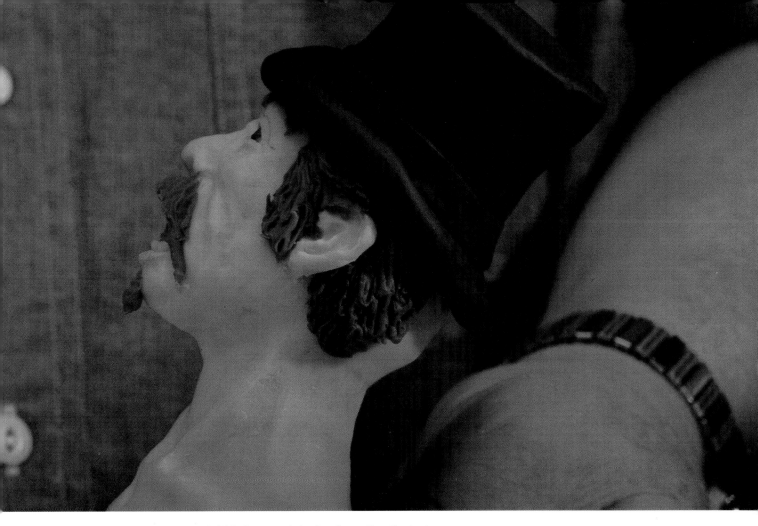

Add hair around the head, creating the texture as you go.

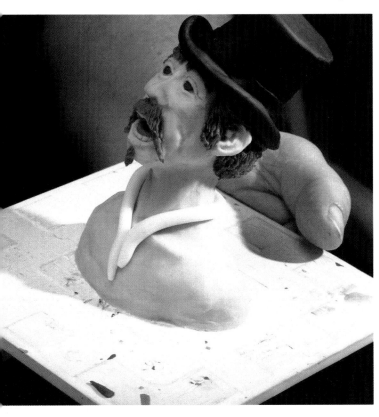

A snake of white...

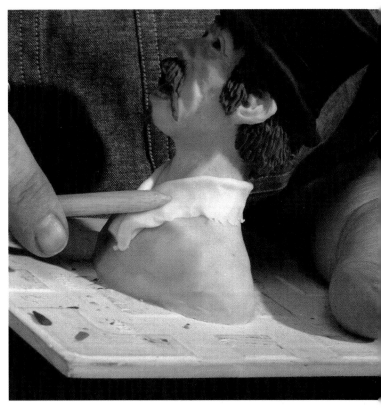

is worked out into a collar.

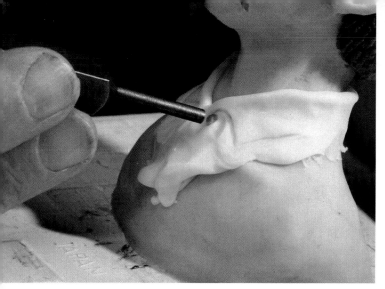

Collar studs can be made with some colored compound in the cup of a nailset.

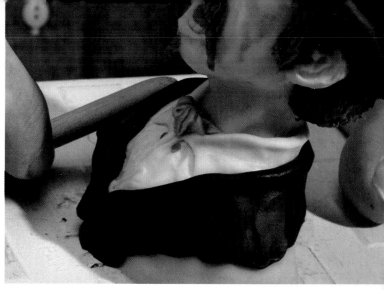

Roll the coat out.

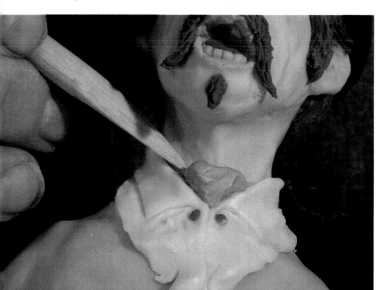

A little blue ascot emerges above the collar and adds to his "dandy" look.

When the coat material covers the torso, establish the line of the collar.

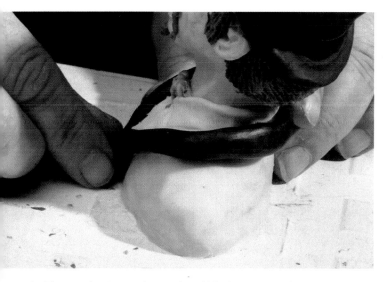

The coat begins with a snake of black compound wrapped around the collar.

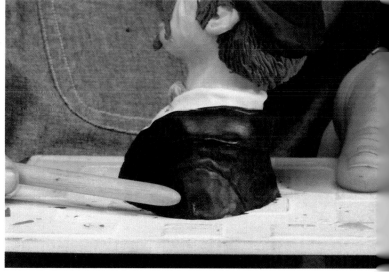

Make a line for a seam at the top of the sleeve.

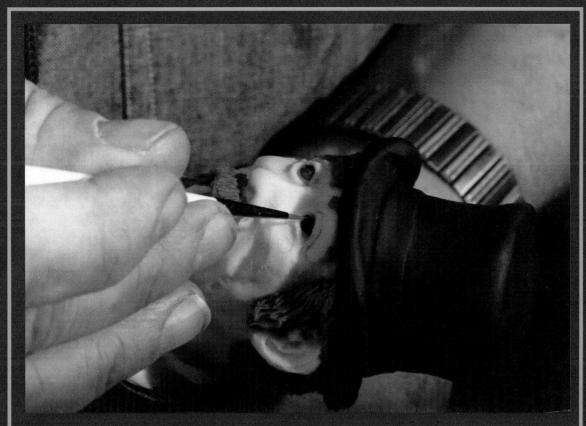

Add a drop of black paint to the eye for the pupil.

The result.

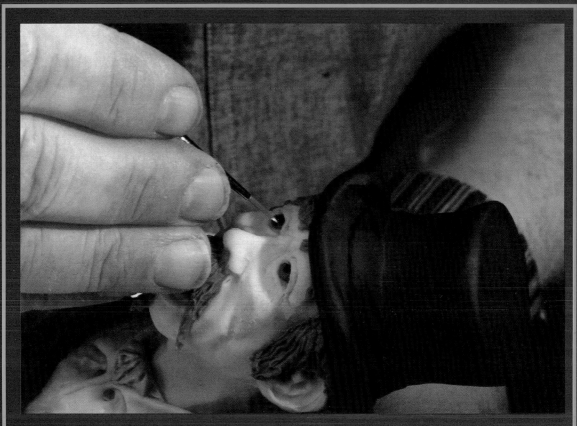

Add a white glint at the same position in each eye.

The result.

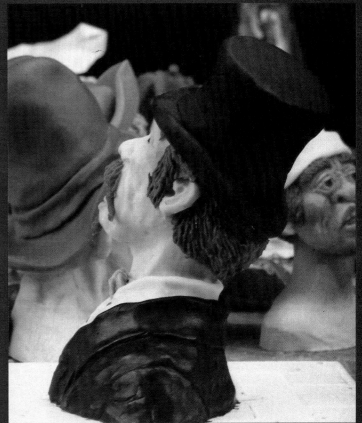

Finished.

The Gallery

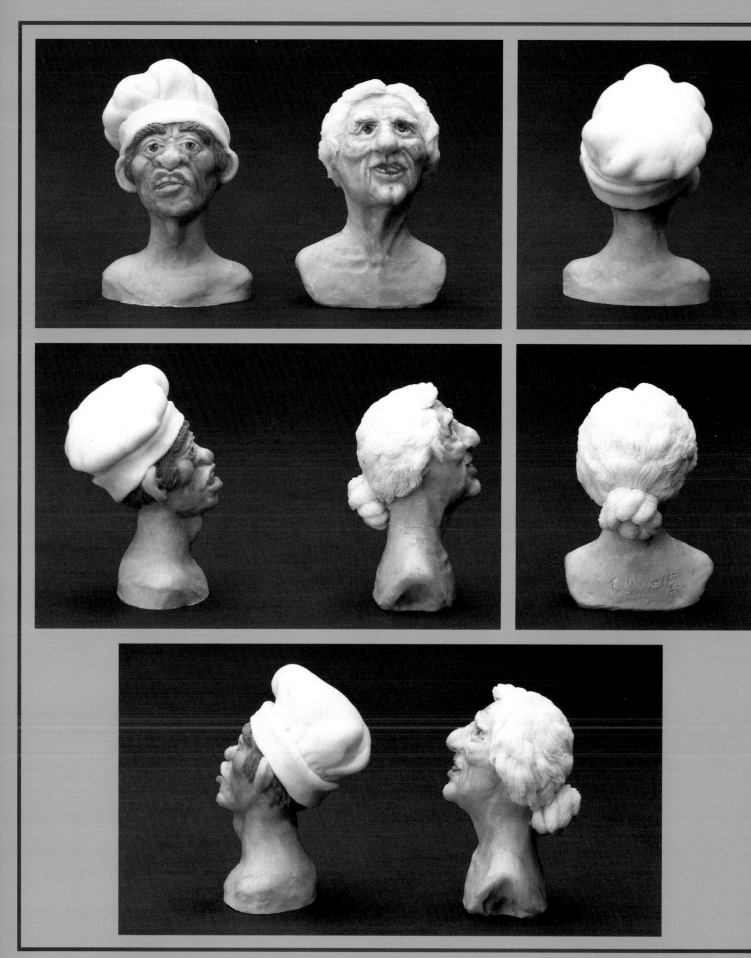